JUST MY WORD

Jordan Winston

JUST MY WORD

Copyright © 2016 by Jordan Winston

All rights reserved. No part of this book may be reproduced or transmitted in any form or by any means without written permission from the author.

ISBN (978-0692724538)

Printed in USA

Dedication

I dedicate this book to every person I have encountered in my life, because without them, this book would not be possible,

With love,
~Jordan

Table of Contents

JUST MY WORD	1
Foreword	9
Preface	10
Introduction	11
Awaken	12
Late Nights	13
How Much I Love You	15
The Word Peach	16
You Need Me	17
1st Lady	18
Why	19
Love Don't Change	20
Shame & Love	21
Two Hearts	21
King & Queen	22
Ally	22
Empire	23
Swelling	24
Alone	26
Baller	27
Turmoil	29
1st Car	30
Life	31
A Winston	38
Simplicity	38
Music Helps	39
Ode to Winter	40
My Mother	41
Money	42
Confucius	43
Words Unsaid	44
Oh Peach	45
Mother & Son Connection	46

Lovers Remembered	47
Critter Adventure	48
Dream Girl	49
Ms. Perfect	49
08 BMW 335i Twin Turbo	50
Black Knight?	51
Cuffing Season	52
Achieve the Impossible featuring Kimberly Wade	53
Abandoned	54
Possible Dorm Raid	55
Ball Is Life	55
Boredom	55
Perplexed Life	56
Peaceful Times	57
Never Alone	58
Darkest Artist	59
Fallen Below	59
Been Too Long	60
Fear to Go	62
Dark Times	62
J.O.R.D.A.N.	63
Openness	63
Journey	63
Independent	64
Right My Wrongs	66
Mistakes	66
Jordan Winston	67
Stop with Rules	68
Vasodepressor Syncope	71
Friends?	72
Friendless	72
Forgive The Past	73
Past Love	73
Missing Love	73

Foreplay	74
Forgotten	75
Heartless Creature	76
Hoodwinked	77
Gone Again	77
Want to be a favorite?	77
Crab Boil	78
Age	79
Cheater's Advice	80
Unfaithful Lifestyle	80
My Mom	81
Mother's Come Up	82
Next Einstein?	82
Military Retirement	83
Mesmerized Eyes	84
Georgia's Fall	85
The Return	86
Appearing Rainbow	87
Untold Relation	87
Baller Comeback	88
Loveless Money	88
Feeling	89
Me	90
Trust Love	91
Old Friend's Return	92
Unexpected Change	92
Judgement Day	93
The One	94
Empty Connections	95
Arizona Rain	96
Endless Options	97
Root of Evil	98
Tricked Girls	98
Efforts Unseen	99

Good Hearted	100
Bad Connection	100
Future Endeavors featuring Kimberly Wade	101
Writer's Block	102
Blind Eyes (Veteran's Day)	103
Overtime	104
Damaged Time	105
In The Rain	106
Legend	107
Done	109
Faithfully Following	110
Wrongful Games	111
Sorry For The Games	111
First Time	112
Past, Present, Future	114
Miles For Your Love	115
Rhonda Rousey & Paris	116
Man Above	117
Drought Season	118
Leeches	119
Focused	120
Unwanted Feelings	121
Blowfish ER Trip	122
Wisdom	123
Single Holidays	123
Swarming Love	124
Unfinished Business	125
Struggle of Passion	126
M.I.G.U.E.L.	127
W.I.N.S.T.O.N.	127
C.A.D.E.N.	128
C.A.M.E.R.O.N.	128
J.A.X.O.N.	128
Study Help	129

End of the Road	130
Do I Want To Have A Stepson	131
I Don't Get Mad	132
Steps To A Happy Broken Heart	135
Lost Body	136
Torn	136
Heart	136
No Feelings	137
Your Love	137
Pieces Of A Heart	137
Blast From The Past	139
Apology	140
Broken	141

Foreword

In the beginning, I had already unfairly profiled him as a young boy destined for greatness; because he was my Son; my firstborn. With wisdom pouring out of him at the tender age of five, he was no ordinary kid. He played hard, but loved harder. He was overly courteous and thoughtful to others. Q&A with him was quite intuitive, yet intriguing.

As a young man, Jordan was very reserved and often secluded himself in his room behind music, television shows or video games. I wasn't sure whether to feel relief or disappointment; relief, because he wasn't out in the world surrounded by immoral behaviors and poor choices, or disappointment, because his social life wasn't escalating as I imagined it would at that point in his life. But somehow, he never lacked in the social department. On the contrary, he was very much a social butterfly in the public eye; with wisdom and good manners in tow. Everyone always complimented me on how mature Jordan was for his age. He was a phenomenal young man; and quite intelligent, also. He seldom studied but always made the grades. I never could figure that out.

And now he's all grown up; full of wisdom, discernment, and poetry. The results of the seclusion he subjected himself to over the years has been poured into this book of poetry. It's personal, it's relatable, and it's his story; some of which I, myself, was introduced to through this book. It's philosophical and moving; a very important accomplishment in his adult life. Here's to manhood...

-Mrs. Kimberly Y. Wade

Preface

My first poem was written long ago. At that time, a book was nowhere in sight, and I was only writing to try something new. The first poem was influenced from music. Music was always the motivating factor that pushed me to write. Music plays a vital role in my everyday life. Though I am not the best singer in the world, I could write poetry to warm a heart. I love music; music is poetry. The challenge to write different styles of poems was even more motivating. The challenge to accomplish over a hundred different types of poetry is what pushed me over the limit to write more. The idea of developing a book did not come to mind, until my mother mentioned it after I was twenty or so poems deep. When she gave me the idea, I ran with it and wrote feverously. After over a hundred poems had been written, the development of the book came.

Introduction

Just My Word is a life experience in such a short book. The book is filled with so much emotion through every page. Every word has a special attachment to life. Every poem has a meaning to be understood, a question to be answered. At least one poem should have an emotional attachment to the heart or soul. The purpose of this book was to express how I feel through poetry. Every word written is poured out from my heart and speaks nothing but the truth. Hopefully, my words can reach out to a heart or soul to change someone's life for the better. People need to realize that life goes on no matter the circumstances and that anything is possible. I am sure my English teachers would have never guessed that I could write poetry in this way but look what we have here. Hopefully, my poems can inspire others to do greater things.

Awaken

As you open your eyes today
You need that motivation to get you up
That encouragement to make it through the day
So know you were awaken with a purpose
Not a purpose to give up
But a purpose to keep striving for the best
Believe today is your day to shine
No time to complain
Take control of your day so you can reign

Late Nights

On these late nights, I sit here and wonder if I will hear your voice
Lonely, cold nights are so lame
Only sitting up to play a simple game
I simply have no other choice
Our conversations have been ending early instead of late
I feel like we have put up a wooden gate
Sometimes I just want to step over that gate with nothing to say
Just to have you in my presence to call you my love
When we have our long conversations, I feel like a stove
All warm and cozy for food being cooked
Our Super Bowl weekend should be booked
But I sit here without any plan or effort to be with you
I think of you when I am on the lou
Just to think of all the things I can't do for you
You are like my little princess waiting for her prince to take control
But that prince sits around like a troll
Fat, Lazy, No Brain
These Late Nights should be filled with fun and joy
A smile should be upon your face every time before you go to sleep
Soon that prince will step up to the plate

You continue to wait, but I wonder for how long
That worries me on these Late Nights
Worries me that someone else is putting that smile on your face
I hope I am not so blind to see the loose lace
Late Nights will soon be ours to conquer once more
Those Nights will be ours once again
Late Nights Late Nights Late Nights

How Much I Love You

Wifey, My Love for you is forever lasting
You are truly one of a kind
My Love for you burns like the sun, ever-lasting
There is only one difference between the sun and my love for you
The sun will burn out sometime far, far in the future
But my Love for you will be for an eternity
Whether on this earth or up in the Heaven
You will always have a special place in my heart
You continue to ask me how much I love you
But I can never really truly tell you exactly how much I love you
There is no explainable definition for the love I have for you
I want you to forever be my best friend no matter what we go through
One Day I hope to make you my wife
But we have to live out our life first
I don't know what to expect out of this world
But I do know that I want you to be there to experience life with me
You are my first love and I hope my last
That is how much I love you

The Word Peach

The word peach is mysterious
Shady and sweet, full of
Motivating spirits, and cherishing taste
Out-pouring into the mouth and taunting like a dream
Forgiving skin
Succulent, smooth, gushing
Juice, with soft lips
Answer
Then question, mouth and body
Of deceit

You Need Me

The girl of my dreams lay asleep in my bed
Yet, I am outside in my car feeling weak
She knows exactly how I feel about her every week
And that is why I think she is here
She is not interested in my kind though
She likes a gap between them thighs
So I am simply just a friend
Even though my feelings are strong
All I can do is play along
She hurts inside and is very insecure
I try my best to comfort her
But maybe my time has not come
My feelings may fade
I wish I just had the chance to be her Ace of Spade
I am patient though
The journey may be tough, but if she is meant to be, my time will come
I am in no rush
No need to push
She is what I've been looking for
I just didn't expect her in this way
But she needs me as much as I need her
How will I ever show you how much we need each other?

1st Lady

The 1st lady in my life
The 1st love of my life
Need someone like her to make my wife
She is forever there in my time of need
Don't ever have to plead
She knows I'll buy her the world
Yet she settles for the simple things
She keeps my head focused
Even when I'm thinking crazy
No doubt I be in a daze
My head is like a maze
But she knows the pattern
She figures out the solution every time
She is truly mine
No one can ever replace her
Not today, not next week or next year
I love this lady
I love you mom

Why

I simply do not understand
You really want me to be your man
You would do anything for me
You would give me your heartbeat
But I just want you to take a seat
I don't see what you see
But you could possibly be my everything
Maybe the distance has me blind
Or maybe I've just made up my mind
You see Mr. Perfect, but I don't see the same
I see a possibility not a perfect match
Maybe I'll just keep watch
I'm not looking for the fame
Just someone that can be my best friend
My thoughts are unclear
You still have me near
Only distance I fear
We'll see it to the end
You just have to make me understand why
Before I die

Love Don't Change

Why do you continue to hide?
I just want you to ride
Do you hate me? Are you scared?
I don't want to be feared
One day you want to talk to me, but not the next day
I want to help you in every way
I wanted to marry you by the bay
But you always fight me away
I'll always be there for you
I wrote some freaking poems for you
We started to build a dream team
Only to get beat in the second round by the dream team
You didn't want to rebuild but I wanted success
Rebuilding is a tough process
I don't like losses, but I'm willing to stack
I want our dream team back
What can I do to get us on track?

Shame & Love

Shameless

I have no fear

I will always be there

Will you let me make it up here?

Do not want to have tears?

Let us be clear

Loveless

Two Hearts

She now has two hearts

How could she be so stingy?

A heartless man waits

May I have my heart back?

Everyone should have one

Love is needed

Even when you were heartless

She still received love

She never could believe.

King & Queen

King
Faithful, Strong
Providing, Loving, Spoiling
The Queen's Strength, The King's Weakness
Caring, Sacrificing, Hardworking
Loyal, Thoughtful
Queen

Ally

The Queen in my eyes
To her I would never lie
With her I will rise

Empire

My empire coexists with a tall five
No one will ever be able to switch
Everybody tries to push me to strive
My fam will never see me as a mitch
Kim is the tall queen of this empire
I am the first tall prince to take the front
Caden is the next tall prince with fire
Cam is the first tall princess on the hunt
Jaxon the tall baby prince will take lead
Only our minds can stop us from success
The smooth dream we have will never be dead
This empire was built with a long process
Tim has helped create the greatest dream team
Now the empire strives for the greatest dream

Swelling

You have been on my mind non-stop since the other one
You could not have thought I was done
You deserve so much better
You deserve so much more
As my heart continues to swell, only love for you reigns
I can't wait to hold you again
I want to throw you in the sky even though you hate it
I continue to write because it is only right
No matter how much I write
The amount of love I have for you will never fit in just one poem
I will never receive the closure I need with these poems
They will never be good enough for you
You are so special and unique
When someone is so close to my heart like you are
You deserve everything
Nothing less than the finest things
I feel like I'll never live up to your standards
Even though you only want success
I feel like that is a long process
My mind always seems to roam
My heart overflows with love like an ice cream cone
I wish you were here
I would give the world to you

But all you want is for me to be better than you
Your heart is large
My heart is only subpar
How will I ever amount to the greatness and happiness you have?

Alone

In the desert all alone
Without a simple call on the phone
Who shall come around prepared?
Do not know why they are scared?

Red is so brave or stupid
She thinks she has been hit by cupid
She believes there is love
Has she come from above?

Rainbow is so funny or sly
She does not care if I die
She believes I have fame
Is she only here to run game?

White is so confused or smart
She thinks she can play a part
She believes I'm the one
Does she know I'm not done?

A few have came, but is one right?
The sun still shines bright
The desert may provide
Just waiting for one to hop in my ride

Baller

The ball hits the court day and night
Others are home at rest
While I practice to shine bright
The dream will soon be a test
Put all the eggs in this nest
Soon to be a shot caller
I will be the best
Because I am a baller

The game never stops right?
Ain't got no time for the breast
Not even one in sight
They nothing but a mess
Simply some distracting stress
They just want to catch a dollar
Trying to be a part of my set
Because I'm a baller

Not trying to be a knight
Trying to become greatness
Just building up my might
No need for my bird chest
Trying to get built up like a treasure chest
Almost sat around and became a roller

No need for a reset
Because I'm a baller

With all the people I have met
People will soon be followers
I'll leave a fancy crest
Because I'm a baller

Turmoil

Once an excited young man to see the world
Dreams were given by a simple paper
That opportunity came and was gone
Plans crushed to step on foreign country's land
Guess traveling will start stateside in style
Close to going up northeast this weekend
Small turmoil flew out all over the place
So now I simply wait for my next chance

1st Car

Are you my shooting star?
Echo - Car
You are here at last
Echo - Fast
What does it seem?
Echo - Beam
You'll be in the family till you're dead
Echo - Red
We will travel all over
Echo - Lover
What will your name be?
Echo - She

Life

Once a young boy striving in school
His only dream was to make it to the NBA
Dreams were huge for this boy
His life was basketball and grades
Work in school was a breeze
He was always above the rest
Thought no practice was ever needed
His height was enough, he thought
Striving through the little leagues
He never tried to improve his game
He only sat around to play video games
No one could stop him
So he believed his dream was near
Even though he was a star young
He never acted like he was the best
Simply played and stayed positive
He encouraged the rest to push
A true motivator within
Never too shy to talk to anyone
His words were always uplifting
Life could not have been better
This boy was getting everything
His parents showed the most love
When no one thought life could get better

A baby boy was born
This young boy had a little brother
Someone to teach him all his ways
Someone to be successful like him
The young boy was so excited
His baby bro practically lived with him
The baby was always sleeping with him
Their bond seemed unbreakable
The young boy was so protective
And always wanted the baby near
With a baby bro in the rear view
Success was the only goal
He wanted to give his bro an idol
The smile on the baby's face was enough
The young boy only wanted better
His grades grew
His stats got padded
He was shining for his lil bro
What more could be done?
He wasn't financially ready
So all he could do was be a role model
Does the baby know what is going on?
Maybe not at the time
But as the baby grew
Hopefully he realizes everything
The young boy only wants what is best
No one will ever replace his first brother

So the young boy thought
Two years later was another birth
But not a boy
It was a girl
The young boy had a girl
Someone he knew he had to protect
He does not know what to teach her
She is not like him
She cannot be too tough or boy like
The young boy realized she was different
She was not able to sleep with the boy
Cause she was a girl
The young boy did not understand
He quickly became a little distant
He continued to cater to his brother
The young boy had to teach his brother
The baby brother had to learn
Learn the ways of protection
The young boy feared one getting hurt
He carefully watched the two everywhere
When the baby bro would hit baby sis
The baby bro got in trouble by big bro
Big bro did not like what he saw
Baby bro was not treated that way
Big bro quickly taught
Baby bro never truly got it though
Baby bro and sis would always fight

The young boy did not like it
But he could not control it
As time passed
Both grew up
Fights continued
And the young boy became distant
Not because of basketball
But because of video games
The young boy was not a star anymore
He still had the grades
But everyone around him knew
That young boy changed
    That young boy became a young man
His mindset finally caught up
He noticed he was not the tallest
He noticed his game was not the best
The young man tried to practice
But video games had him stuck
His grades were still on point
But his dreams were fading
The effort to practice was not there
His dreams remained
But his drive was not the same
The motivation was there
He felt he did not need the practice
All his friends were ready for tryouts
Not the little leagues

Time for middle school ball
Luckily, the young man was moving
So he skipped the tryouts
He was scared of failure
And he thought he would be gone soon
The young man did not leave soon
He missed out on a whole season
He could have easily made the team
But he was unprepared
He even broke up with his girl early
The young man was ready to go
Ready to change his ways
Start fresh somewhere else
He finally moved away
Thinking that things would be better
He lost all his friends though
The new area was not his comfort zone
The young man was lost
His grades did not drop though
And he did make the basketball team
Maybe it was the height
Or maybe his skills
No one knows
His talent was so raw and undeveloped
Yet, no one was there to develop
This young man sat and rotted
Talents and height being wasted

A friend close to my family tried
But he was turned away
Why he was turned away
The young man will never know
Every year he made friends
He made the grades
He made the teams
But he was not the star he used to be
Even with a second baby brother
The young man was lazy
And continued to play video games
He let the dream fade
The young man always thought positive
Thought he was good enough to make it
He was told he should practice
He only ignored the comments
He went through the years making teams
Yet, he would get kicked off
His attitude was too big
No one wanted to deal with it
No one wanted to fight through it
He was not helped into college
He had the grades
But not the skill
The young man never worried
He knew he had the military to go to
So that was the path he took

Off to the Air Force
With an attitude like his
No one knows how he made it
He had minor setbacks
Yet, he still made it
This young man became an adult
And within the Air Force
His dream lived on
His dream to make it to the NBA
He plans to start at the base team
Then get to the Air Force team
Practice was done
He got better and better
One week away from tryouts
But the man finds out some news
His heart was not able
The dream may be dead
Basketball may no longer be life
He might not achieve that dream
But he did achieve one dream
The dream of a role model to his siblings

A Winston

Man, history shows it all,
That every Winston will fall,
But if I fight for the prize,
I can prove to the world a Winston can rise

Simplicity

Life is so simple
Play your part like a dimple
Don't be a pimple

Music Helps

Listening to music day and night

Only a Wednesday but it has been so chill

Without music I would not be right

The sound to my ears keeps me trill

Not much time left in the week

But music will carry me through

Does not always have to be Drake

But he definitely keeps me at my peak

The sound makes no situation rough

Always good in a wake and bake

Ode to Winter

Cold Winter, you sit just around the corner
Your weather makes everyone want to cuddle
You're the opposite of summer
No need for any puddles
Your days are so relaxing and calm
Brings everyone close
Snowflakes fall to my palm
This season is not like most
No more yard work
Nothing but enjoying the beautiful indoors
Does the winter bring out peace?
Or a fake piece?
Give me a reason
Winter is the best season

My Mother

Love-Giver
Peace-Maker
Christian-Lover

Discipline-Giver
Family-Maker
Cook-Lover
Care-Provider

Hug-Giver
Success-Maker
Kid-Lover
Height-Hater

The Best Around
My Mom

Money

Without money, what would this world be?
Nothing would ever have a fee
But money has taken a crazy path
Don't let money give you wrath

Money is about the source to everything
Only money can get you that ring
All you have to do is be good at math
Don't let money give you wrath

Money can make your life happy
Also can quickly make life nappy
Make money your craft
Don't let money give you wrath

Control all of your money
Don't be caught looking like a dummy
Be discipline with a lash
Don't let money give you wrath

Confucius

There was a girl who stays confused
Her name is Ms. Perfect without any clue
She continues to hide
Why won't she just take a ride?
Instead she only leaves me with the blues

Words Unsaid

You left me here with a few poems
A few thoughts unknown
A few words unsaid
What am I supposed to think?
Treat You Like Somebody like Tink
I feel we need to talk
But yet, I haven't took the walk
I'd rather text you
Then come and see you
Why? Cause I feel like you bs me
I just want to know how you feel about me
Your poems give hints
But your actions leave dents
If you're really wondering
Why aren't you trying?

Oh Peach

Oh Peach,
You are soft to the touch like snow,
The color of your skin shines bright
And as peachy as the yellow sun.
I love the juices that flow like a river
However, you can be dry as a drought.
Peach, small, succulent Peach
How I love to hold you like a newborn baby
Don't know how my nights would be spent without you
Oh Peach,
None have quite been like you, none at all,
Your fruit is made for guys who act as kings
Nevertheless, you are mine, oh Peach!

Mother & Son Connection

Our souls are interconnected together
Our hearts are so caring for everyone here
No matter the time of day or the weather
We are always there for the ones that are near
Our hugs are always as soft as a feather
Everyone understands our love is so clear
This connection can never ever break
As long as we stay calm and listen to Drake

Lovers Remembered

Remember those who we truly love
They will never be forgotten
They don't go away like a dove
So don't treat them like they are rotten

They will never be forgotten
Your mind can only be distracted
So don't treat them like they are rotten
Aggression is so overrated

Your mind can only be distracted
Treat those you love with respect
Aggression is so overrated
Don't do something you will regret

Treat those you love with respect
They don't go away like a dove
Don't do anything you will regret
Remember those you truly love

Critter Adventure

Get away, you small little critter, leave
And never be found around again
From my room unless you want pain

You are definitely a pet peeve
The way you crawl is not right here
Don't make someone miss you, oh dear,

Now I must deliver you to the heat
You will soon burn like meat
The dryer is where you will lie
The dryer is where you must die
Hopefully, no one will remember you
I'm glad I didn't have to ruin my shoe

Dream Girl

Has she come to me?
The girl of my dreams is back
Is this trickery?

How my mind is so confused
I do not know what to do

Ms. Perfect

She is confused
She is beautiful beyond imagination
She is brown skinned
She has natural gorgeous hair
She wants me?
She is Ms. Perfect?
She is the one

08 BMW 335i Twin Turbo

It is sexy black
Speed it does not lack
It makes me look like a Mack
Can definitely last on the track
Will never be in the back
Always will be in tack
Won't ever be on a rack
My BMW is not whack

Black Knight?

Only if you knew how I felt
The world would be sitting in your lap
Play the cards that you were dealt
Do I need to lay you out a map?
Just want the same love you show Kim
Am I not worth the same love?
Must I pour my heart out?
Do I need to give up a limb?
Maybe you will get my message by dove
Hopefully, you realize I won't pussy out

Cuffing Season

During Cuffing Season we should not be alone
Late nights we should be on the phone
Cuddling up so we can be warm
Hanging out in any form
Definitely the best time to bone

Or sing a nice little tone
Not the weather for a snow cone
Don't want to be alone in this dorm
During Cuffing Season

My love is forever shown
Because the love for me is not known
No one to hold during a storm
This is not the norm
I think my chance was blown
During Cuffing Season

Achieve the Impossible
featuring Kimberly Wade

A Dream is waiting
Something that will be achieved
The only way is up

Impossible it may be
One's actions will supersede

Actions that are hard
But one's hard work will pay off
Just need to have faith

The substance of things hoped for
Success, the evident core

Nothing but the best
No time to mess with the rest
We want nothing less

Nothing less than great success
So we work hard to be blessed

Abandoned

Tonight, I sit on the back of a truck alone
Where did everyone in my life go?
Not even a single text will hit my phone
Why do I feel so low?

Abandoned in a crazy world
Not a soul out worth my love
Leaves me every night uncurled
Just waiting for that beautiful dove

Doves come and show love daily
Even though I come up heartless
Don't want no damn Hailey
Feels like I'm really careless

My life is truly amazing
Don't be fooled by the flu gazey

Possible Dorm Raid

Mysterious help
Came from the darkness around
Good thing I am clean

Ball Is Life

Ball
Is something with life
Not violent like a deadly knife
A sphere filled with the greatest chance
Shooting takes proper stance
Orange ball within fall
Ball

Boredom

Boredom strikes at night
Especially on night shift
No one to talk to
Everything is so draining
Motivation is them bills

Perplexed Life

Hospital trips days and nights
Thoughts through my head that don't make sense
But everything in my life seems right

Seems like I am building a fence
No one out in this world I could trust
Only trust from my mom which is immense

Starting to think my heart is turning to dust
Only God knows what will happen next
I just wait and try not to rust

People feel that my life is not complex
They are only fooled by my peace with God
He taught me to keep my life perplexed

Peaceful Times

Smooth

As a

Summer day

When we had peace

No one had to worry about safety

Never Alone

Do not worry you are never alone
Just some time where you learn to grow
People will not always blow up your phone
Do not worry you are never alone
Sometimes you have to go fetch your bone
Someone will be there if you let them know
Do not worry you are never alone
Just some time where you learn to grow

Darkest Artist

Heartless
Fearless
Thoughtless
Artist
I am a heartless, fearless human
I am the darkest, thoughtless artist

Fallen Below

The darkest artist
Once the smartest
Now he sits below
Why did he fall so low?

Been Too Long

[Verse 1]
Why can't this day come sooner?
Been too many days since I left you
I'm still sitting here missing you
You shoulda visited already
Said I gotta message today
You always know how to make me smile
I just wanted to call you and let you know
Thank you for everything

[Hook]
Momma
I appreciate everything that you do
You took the time to show me
Think it is time for everyone to know
That I thank you

Watch me
Grow into the man you want me to be
Successful and stress free
With no debt
I thank you for everything
Hoo ooh hoh, hoo ooh hoh
You're the best
Always thank you Ooh ooh

Hoo ooh hoh
You're the best
I thank you

[Verse 2]
Can't wait for us to meet again
My heart yearns for your hugs
Hope I don't have to wait too long
I will always be your son
Aggravating you in every way
Cuz no one can replace me
But you know I have to grow up
Just like you, I want to be successful

[Hook]

[Bridge]
Hoh ooh hoh
Hoh ooh hoh
Hoh ooh hoh
Just like you
I want to be successful
Hoh ooh hoh
Hoh ooh hoh
Hoh ooh hoh

[Hook]

Fear to Go

Alone I still sit
No one in my life to hold
Soon I will explore
But where should I even go
This world can be so very cold

Dark Times

Times with me can be so fun
But my personality is a pun
No place for distance
My mind wants no chance
And my heart definitely seems done

J.O.R.D.A.N.

Just
Ordinarily
Robust
Defining
Amazing
Nobility

Openness

Open up to me
Life can be so much better
With me in your life

Journey

A man with a perplexed life
Browsing for someone to have his back
Can anyone deal with his mess?
Does this woman even exist?
Only time will tell on this journey

Independent

At least I'm not like the rest
Branching off in my own mess
Contradicting the family history
Don't worry how I make my living
Exchanging the negative with the positive
Feedback is greatly appreciated
Guaranteed to establish success
History to be made
I will strive to be the best
Jordan is the name to remember
Kimberly is the one who raised a king
Look what society has created
March baby with the brain of a thinker
No time to be bothered by stress
Opportunity is all around this world
Pisces here that will take advantage
Quiet and patient to strike
Raising slowly in a crazy world
Still wondering if I was born to the right generation
Thought process so deep
Understood by no one
Very unlikely to fail
Winston name will prevail
X-rays trying to stop my journey

You'd be dumb to believe that will stop me
Zetetic people will come around to stop me

Right My Wrongs

My personality makes me want a response
No sleep without forgiveness of my wrongdoing
The only way to receive that is to right wrongs
Without understanding, that is impossible
That is why I still seek a perspective from few
Only want to right my wrong to gain peace at heart
This process is hard when you do not understand
How on earth will I be able to right my wrong?

Mistakes

Misunderstandings may make my misfortunes
Taking time to terminate tremors
Cases caused crazy conditions
Wrongs waiting with wrath

Jordan Winston

Jordan

Understanding, Honest, Playful, Caring

Brother of Savion Melton, Darien Harbert, Vinson Winston Jr., Caden, Cameron and Jaxon Wade

Lover of psychology, basketball, people

Who feels blessed, heartless, at peace

Who fears God, God, God

Who would like to see Aubrey Graham, Success, Family

Resident of Atlanta, Georgia

Winston

Stop with Rules

Never fear
Never stop
Stop being afraid
Stop running away
Away I'd like to take you
Away from society
Society cannot win
Society is crazy
Crazy world
Crazy sensation
Sensation for you
Sensation for us
Us means nothing
Us isn't real
Real, I wish
Real, I am
Am I a fool?
Am I the game?
Game I run
Game is fun
Fun till pain
Fun till I'm hurt
Hurt I can be
Hurt to my heart

Heart irregular
Heart on last beat
Beat no one understands
Beat that lets me live
Live in happiness
Live in peace
Peace always here
Peace here within
Within my heart love
Within my brain plays
Plays game no one wants
Plays game without a thought
Thought of fun
Thought of pain
Pain which prevails
Pain that grows
Grows slowly
Grows inside
Inside, I grow
Inside. I'm defective
Defective, I may be
Defective, I will win
Win without any cheat
Win with these rigged rules
Rules where I stand
Rules of a Winston

Winston...
Stand...

Vasodepressor Syncope

What is this serious condition to me?
Nothing, but a label
Still going to drink my dad under the table
Still going to ball cause ball is life
In my eyes, that is only right
Life will not change for anything
Especially if I want a ring
Condition says stay away from warm weather
Good thing me and the heat weren't together
This condition is only progression
About to get my degree in my profession
Vasodepressor Syncope

Friends?

How can you trust them
Snakes right in front of your eyes
Only there when they need you
Not someone that cares
Nothing but leeches in life
No one to actually claim

Friendless

Friends do not exist here
I have my heart filled with fear

No time to be left again
With my heart in pain

I just want someone to trust
Before I turn into dust

Forgive The Past

My Love, come back, don't runaway
Let the past stay in the past
Please forgive me in every way
Let me make you my last

Past Love

Old Times
Memories
Left in the past
With no chance to come back
Past Love

Missing Love

Missing
Your Love in life
Incomplete space in me
Heart was replaced with an ice box
Love

Foreplay

Foreplay
Done four
Kiss, Head, Love
Fun, Amazing, Exciting, Peaceful
Sex

Forgotten

If I were to fade,
If time were to end,
If I was away,
If I disappeared,
Who would truly care?

No one to care
Just me alone
Without loved ones
In my despair

Who is here?
Where am I?
What am I?

No one
Even cares

Forgotten

Heartless Creature

Life on this earth makes me truly wonder
Who I can count on in my time of need
No one in clear range when I hear thunder
But they swarm near when it is time to feed
And I blindly fill the bellies of greed

Only to find them gone when they are full
Taking advantage of me like a mull
Keeping me away from the next leecher
But they don't realize they made me a bull
Within now I feel a heartless creature

Hoodwinked

Believed I had found the one
Only to look like a clown
Like God said, "She was for you"
Then I heard..."Got'Em?"

Gone Again

You decided to hit my phone today
Only to realize the memory of you was lost
Because you decided to not pay the cost
So again you just went away

Want to be a favorite?

You say you wanna be somebody's favorite
Yet you curve everybody who wants to date it...

Crab Boil

Seafood is such a delight
Crabs increase the fight
Shrimp scampi must be in sight
Sausage cooked just right
Corn to strengthen might
That first bite
Tight

Age

Age,

Time gap

Where you grow

Because you learn.

You make decisions

For the best or the worst

To experience your life

To live the story parents told.

Kids want to become adults so fast

Yet they miss their young days when they are old

Cheater's Advice

Somebody popped in my inbox this morning
Trying to get advice so she can get this ring
She cheated because her man cheated
Told her that logic was conceited
Quickly gave my advice with no suspense
If messages were heard, there would be silence

Unfaithful Lifestyle

Unfaithful lifestyle
Gives you temporary love
But leaves you alone

My Mom

My mom
My calm

Her fight
My might

She plan
I ran

To live
She give

Success
Void less

Mother's Come Up

Brought into this world a new life
Without a man to claim her as a wife
Yet she still handled business to get out the hood
Only now to be happy and living good

Next Einstein?

Genius at heart
Or book smart by the brains
You are nothing but a piece of art
Living with aged pains

Military Retirement

The end of my career is near
Time for me to go back to school
Gotta hit these books with no fear
Don't want to end up like a fool

Plans on what I want to do made
Trying not to waste too much time
Ain't trying to hear all the shade
Success will begin with my climb

First I must enroll in college
Quickly get out my parent's home
To begin to gain this knowledge
Might get that if I go to Rome

But what college perfects my niche?
This retirement won't make me rich

Mesmerized Eyes

Tonight I believe I saw you
Pulling in the parking lot as I was leaving
Were you coming to see me?
Cause you don't live there
Was that you or was my eyes mesmerized?
All I could do was watch
Wasn't going to turn around for you
You're only playing a childish game
Just like I use to do
Yet you still on my mind hours later
What do you want from me?
I gave you whatever and you still played
You could have been the one
But I couldn't figure out the cheats to the game you was playing

Georgia's Fall

Miss the days of that country breeze
Driving through a tunnel of fallen leaves
Fall brings out a beautiful scene
Even on a night like Halloween
The area shines like a citrine

The Return

In my never-ending thought process
You do not observe what I observe
A mean little girl with a body somewhat pure
Wanting to be claimed by someone who is fading
At least that was your mindset before
Now you are back home with options around
You do not act the same
Like I so clearly pointed out

In my tentative eyes
I pay attention to all things around me
So of course I see through the game you were playing
Now that you have returned
I'll only fade away until I become...
A distant memory...

Appearing Rainbow

Why can't you just become a distant memory?
You didn't have to text me
You say you want nothing to do with me
Yet you try to sneak back endlessly
Only to reveal again our connection is empty
Just leave me alone
So my mind can be set free
And I stop dreaming of these fantasies

But you are so beautiful to the touch
There was never a dull moment
At least I didn't see it much
Guess I was missing a component
These girls made me Nonesuch
Just wish I could keep you more than content

Untold Relation

Wanted to be your best friend
But you wanted something else
Friendship faded way too soon
We could have had a lot of fun

Baller Comeback

Once was a baller
Sidelined by my heart
Need to get back right
To go get this ring

Loveless Money

Why does everybody want to be loved?
Forget this love talk for now
Let's talk on this money

Feeling

Maybe feelings should be my middle name

My mind is always deep in them

Forever thinkin of what could have been

Even the ones I was never in

Me and Drake just might be kin

Mind forever roaming around bad trust issues

Might end up a human so vicious

Me

I'm
Living
Successful
Without problems
Me

Trust Love

Threat to our heart?
Forget about love
Yet love we desire
Preset by the man above

Why is love so tough?
Comply with love we must
Supply all the love we can
Thereby we may trust

Old Friend's Return

This old friend reached out to me today
Haven't heard from her since I went away
She thinks we have not changed
I think she may be deranged
But for now I will play her way

Unexpected Change

Here I sit a few hours to hear the results for the rest of my life....

Judgement Day

Yesterday I made sure to pray

Cause I knew the next morning was the day

The day I find out whether I go or stay

My mind has been wondering everyday

Plans already made if I must go away

All I can do is obey

I have no say

Soon my life plans will be on display

No time for me to go astray

Never know when I will decay

The One

One
Will come
Soon enough
For me to love
Even if years pass
My love will come
Because she
Is the
Only
One

Empty Connections

Why am I always in my feelings?
Always thinking of what could be
Even though nothing is there
My mind still wonders why
Brain never stopping
I need someone
To hold me
Down till
Death

Arizona Rain

The rain rushes your car with no fear
Only to leave your car with dust
The rain dries itself off to look like rust
To look me in the eye to see my tear

Endless Options

So many girls, but is there one?
Options endless but efforts ghost
Where in the world will I find one?
She must be right along the coast

Or maybe we haven't met yet
So many girls, but is there one?
All these girls seem to be undone
Filled with regret they can't forget

Girls quick to say they done with guys
Just to find out girls ain't no prize
So many girls, but is there one?
Man this fun has only begun

Ain't no worries to find the one
With one of these I will have won
Hopefully to carry my son
So many girls, but is there one?

Root of Evil

Crazy Money
Everybody needs
Why can't things just be free?

Tricked Girls

Women want me
Yet, I play all games
Why are girls mesmerized?

Efforts Unseen

Wrote these essays today for three girls
Just wanted them to know how I truly feel
Hoping to get a clear understanding
Yet they only gave my mind the swirls
Nobody feels the way I feel
Maybe I'm just too demanding
No girl seems to really care
Even with all the time I have put in
A relationship with me: they wouldn't dare
I'm lost in this world like hay with a pin

Good Hearted

Never can walk past a girl in tears
Her next step is what I truly fear
Have to show her at least one person cares
Before she does something severe
If not me, who would interfere?

Bad Connection

Not much love for the ones I want
They all just seem like a mere taunt
The connection is never strong
Because I end up doing wrong
Something I never try to flaunt

Future Endeavors featuring Kimberly Wade

The start has been so-so
But with age we definitely grow
Now is the time to go

While the road may be long
It's the journey that makes us strong

Even when times get rough
We must continue to fight and trust
Our faith is enough

So while others may doubt
We will definitely work it out
Too much opportunity to be without

We must take advantage to be the best
Otherwise we will look like the rest

Our future endeavors won't be denied
Dreams turned into plans and plans will take flight
All minds are clear and prepared for this ride

Writer's Block

Struggling lately to write
My mind has been on lock
Seems like I lost my talent overnight

Maybe because I don't hear that knock
Or maybe I am too focused with the doc

My heart continues to beat
So I cannot accept defeat

Blind Eyes (Veteran's Day)

Thank You?
No need for thanks
Heroes are all over
My uniform tells you nothing
I could have killed many or none at all
Just appreciate good people
Cause you only see art
Not the efforts
Thank You

Overtime

Every time I believe something may have changed
But that is simply just my mind playing games
Our friendship continues to remain deranged
Maybe this connection should just burn in flames
Cannot force a title that is prearranged
Might just have to abandon this love she claims
Baby these old games are not fun anymore
With all this overtime just let me be yours

Damaged Time

Just like you said before
Maybe this is not meant to be
Seven years is not good enough to thee

Thought in time you would be my boo
Nobody else seems to compare to you
Come to find out you just a kangaroo

Hopping from, "you care about me" to "can't stand me"
Maybe it is just your homosexuality
No relationship for us is what I foresee

Hopefully, you won't stay confused
Definitely don't want you to be used
Tired of trying to keep you amused

In The Rain

In the rain our actions are vile
For now I remain in exile
Hoping one day to have your all
Maybe my time will be next fall
Until then I will run this mile

Just for you to see that cute smile
Even though that might take a while
My body will stay standing tall
In the rain

No matter the fights that compile
One day I hope to reconcile
So I can break down this stonewall
To kiss you under the rainfall
Hopefully to pass this trial
In the rain

Legend

On this path to gain my crown
Days are filled with joy and pain
The criticism won't knock me down
But they gone hate when I start to reign

Many people get where I am and shutdown
Competition gets tough so they complain
The struggle is what I must sustain
On this path to gain my crown

Everybody waiting for me to breakdown
My plan is what I must maintain
Some days I may just drown
Days are filled with joy and pain

People don't see my vision cause of their birdbrain
Not use to having a complex mind around
Their words I do entertain
The criticism won't knock me down

On the rise from my small hometown
No need for my mouth to explain
Everybody thought I was gone be a clown
But they gone hate when I start to reign

This world is just my playground
Definitely not my final domain
Building up for the final showdown
My faith is what I must contain
                      On this path.

Done

Time for me to take my own advice
My love given is underpriced
Bout that time to move on to the next
So I can end up in paradise

That waiting around game dead
Words just gone have to be left unsaid
Fallback game too strong
Just about to focus on chasing this bread

The game's played - you may have won
Remember though you not just losing anyone
Losing the one who cared for you the most
Yes, I'm finally done

Faithfully Following

Only time will tell on this journey ahead
My trust lies faithfully in the man above
Whatever He has planned is where I'm headed
Open-eyed or blind

Wrongful Games

The games played
    never
Seemed to stop no matter
    what
You did in attempt for me.
Your heart is broken.
Yet the games continue on
For no wise explanation

Sorry For The Games

I am sorry dear
My games seem to never end
You are stuck like glue

First Time

Give your love away daily
But never to the right one
Only to someone who gives you temporary fun
When will you open your eyes to see
That the one for you is me?
Simply just need one time

Waiting here so patiently
Yet you still giving second chances
To the ones who cannot see
The beauty you hold within
For the one who wants more than fun
Oh why can't that be me

Passed on the chance to be the one
Felt like we were rushing into something
Seemed a little suspect to me
We didn't even talk daily
So why should I believe the time is right
When you can't even tell me why

No doubt I would love you right the first time
Wouldn't need a second chance
Because in my eyes you are the one

Too bad you don't feel the same
At least that is what my eyes see
Cause my ears seem to be deaf when you speak

Baby, I would love to talk to you daily
So why are you doing this me
Is it because I want more than fun
Or is it cause my feelings show
You say you want to be somebody's only one
However your insecurities overrun

All I need is for one chance
Shower you with love the first time
Just waiting for you to stop your fun
Even if that is possible
Your love could be the one
Or I could be wasting time

Until I have my first time
My mind will think of you daily
Hopefully you will get to see

Past, Present, Future

In the past my mind was blind to the world
Thinking the world owed me everything
Nobody could tell me what to believe
My mind was open to no discussion
The present hit with harsh reality
But my mind stored information
So luckily I was prepared now
To take on this crazy world
In hopes to build a future
For myself and my kids
No turning back now
Must continue on
This wild journey
Everything will
Come to one
As long as I
Start with
No one
Except
Me

Miles For Your Love

I will run miles every day and night for your love to be mine
My heart won't allow me to run though so maybe just a slow jog
Just hope you meet me halfway before I pass out alone

Rhonda Rousey & Paris

Our state of mind cannot be at peace
We have lost something dear to us
Something we don't want to discuss
Someone has torn us apiece

Many hospitalized and many killed
People lost on where to go from here
But they know it is time to build
No time to just disappear

Planning on a time to fight back
They must retaliate on this attack
Must have their payback
Instead of just a setback

Everybody is ready for another fight
However nothing will happen overnight

Man Above

He has always been the one
in my time of need
none compare
to what He has done

He will forever keep my faith within me
instead of losing my hope
my life
will be great
with Him by my side

no one can tell me anything differently
cause they are not Him
and He knows all this life holds

Drought Season

Cleanse my mind and heart of this thought
Don't know what to think on this drought
Mind so unclear

Only here in your time of need
But my actions always succeed
No need for fear

Leeches

Man forget all this
Ain't nobody real no more
People not working
Niggas want a free ticket
Man I'm just gone stick to me

Focused

"Don't take life too seriously
You'll never get out of it alive"
This quote stuck to me mysteriously

Gave me the momentum to survive
Kept me with a peace of mind
Only to continually thrive

My life won't be undefined
I will stay on my grind

Unwanted Feelings

Starting to believe girls are confused
Always cry out that niggas won't open up
But when we try, we get excused

Seems to me like a setup
So niggas tend to hold emotions in
Which eventually leads to a breakup

Then the tears seem to begin
With posts of a nigga being so excess
Yet we only wanted to share what was within

Only to end up in more of a mess
With no sight of success

Blowfish ER Trip

Saturday was chill till you hit me up
Hit my phone with a bad situation
Of course I thought it was all a setup

Needed a little more of an explanation
Never know what to believe when it comes to you
Thought you was just trying to have conversation

Seems to me you just stuck like glue
But all you wanted was somebody near
This time here ain't nothing new

Just wanted my help, that was clear
Everything back to normal the next day
Our bond will again disappear

Glad you were okay anyway
Holiday right around the corner
Wouldn't want no harm this holiday

You sure did look like a foreigner
Saturday was chill till you hit me up
That text message could have been a warner
Of course I thought it was all a setup

Wisdom

Wise
Wisdom
Comes in time
Without the age
People see the wisdom no matter age

Single Holidays

No girl in sight
On the night where
She might find me

Swarming Love

Before your heart evolves into stone,
Let my love enter like a swarm
And take us to what is unknown.
Before your heart evolves into stone,
Your love will be my very own.
Maybe one day we'll pass the storm
Before your heart evolves into stone.
Let my love enter like a swarm.

Unfinished Business

Timeless

Rhymeless

Crimeless

Diamond

My works are timeless, but a diamond

Work so rhymeless? Surprised I'm crimeless?

Struggle of Passion

In my heart, passion is what I must feel
When the start of my dreams is overdue
The struggle has always been real

Late starts tend to be a big ordeal
My dream is still what I must pursue
In my heart, passion is what I must feel

Passion is what I must reveal
This challenge must be a preview
The struggle has always been real

Opportunity in my face that I must steal
No time to stop, must see my plan through
In my heart, passion is what I must feel

Starting my plans now is ideal
Soon to make my college debut
The struggle has always been real

My life right now seems all surreal
But I can very well make it all true
In my heart, passion is what I must feel
The struggle has always been real.

M.I.G.U.E.L.

Mauerbauertraurigkeit

Intriguing

Genuine

Unique

Emotional

Loyal

W.I.N.S.T.O.N.

Wise

Imaginative

Natural

Social

Tentative

Opportunist

Nice

C.A.D.E.N.

Can he be the next Cam Newton
And have the brain of Einstein?
Does he know his potential is sky high?
Everything will not come easy though
No time to waste if you want to be King

C.A.M.E.R.O.N.

Competitiveness is in her blood
A young girl striving for the finest things
Motivation must always stay high
Even as the time flies by
Remember you have the keys to your dreams
Opportunist is what you must be
No one can stop you from being a Queen

J.A.X.O.N.

Just waiting on the year you can play sports
A big boy ready to take the world by storm
X-Factor you will be on any team
Obviously better than the rest
Never give up on your dreams

Study Help

Once again you have come and go
Only talk to me when you're in need
Asking for your time is what I no longer plead
When you come and go, I no longer feel low

End of the Road

Once upon a time, I thought you were the one
Thought we would never be done
But you chose a different path
Really thought you were going to be someone

Someone who would prove me wrong
Someone who could tag along
Yet you took the wrong turn
And showed me that you don't belong

Our relationship never really flowed
Always just seemed like an extra load
Now the time has come
Because this is the end of the road

Do I Want To Have A Stepson

An old friend has appeared back in my life
She claims she has always wanted to be my wife
But she has come back with a son
Do I want to have a stepson?

This woman is making herself sound perfect for me
But her child is the only thing I see
That child cannot be undone
Do I want to have a stepson?

She wants to be a part of my team
But she isn't the girl of my dream
That child cannot be outrun
Do I want to have a stepson?

All kids have my heart
But is that how my family should start?
My mind is only trying to have fun
Do I want to have a stepson?

For now I'll play the game
Maybe she will make me feel the same
My kid count is at none
Do I want to have a stepson?

I Don't Get Mad

[Intro]
Girl all in my face
What the hell she think she doing?
Tryna hit me wit some mace
What the hell she trying to do?

[Verse 1]
She start snapping and going off
She blowin' up my freakin' phone
I'm so chill and freakin' calm
I know that I'm da bomb
She asked why I wasn't mad
I told her I'm like my dad
She told me that might be bad
Wasn't worried I don't get mad
She freaked out that ruined her plans
I told her to calm down cause I am the freakin' man
Baby listen up, you'll only hear this one time
I just want to tell you that....

[Chorus x2]
I don't get mad, I don't get mad
Dadadaaaaa Dadadaaaaa lalalaaaaa
I don't get mad, I don't get mad

Baby I will never be pissed
I only want to be missed
You could put my heart on lockdown
But you only trying to break me down
It's ok it's alright cause...

[Verse 2]
I don't get mad you don't open up
Soon I will have had enough
I will make you mine forever
Gain the keys to your heart
You have calmed down and let me in
Let me tell you it wasn't easy, it's been a good minute
I put in the time, I put in the work
I almost feel like a dork
But you're worth it, you're finally mine
Now it's time to stay on my grind
Continue to make you happy
So I get that sloppy toppy(*Male laughter*)

[Chorus x2]

[Closing]
My mind is at peace
You control the beast in me
As long as you are by my side
I don't get mad, I don't get mad

Dadadaaaaa Dadadaaaaa lalalaaaaa
I don't get mad, I don't get mad

Steps To A Happy Broken Heart

To become heartbroken
And still laugh through pain
Follow this path
So you don't end with wrath

Lies
Lies you will always hear
Protect your heart from things not dear
Don't let lies be something you fear

Laugh
Don't take life so seriously
Step back and laugh at the pain
Laughing can keep you from going insane

Love
Love your life when you are alone
Know what you are feeling is not lust
Hold your heart near you must

Peace
Find what keeps you calm
A reliable source always in reach
Without peace, you cannot teach

Lost Body

Once a heart so broken down
Built up to last the storm
Only to see you finally drown
Body dead, it will never return to form

Torn

How could your eyes be so blind?
My absence lead to morals lost
Hope that lust was worth the cost
My presence you will never find

Heart

Heart,
My life,
You teach me
Feelings daily
With planned reactions.
What is your plan in me?
To take on pain before love?
Or show my soul what I'm blind to?
Mindset not complimenting the heart
A lesson must definitely be taught

No Feelings

For someone to love another person,
The actions shown definitely differ.
How could you love when your heart and soul don't agree?
Glad my mind told me not to listen
Words spoken didn't match your soul
With what you did, you have no feelings for me
Everything I said came true, but you're too blind to see
Glad my broken heart avoided that knife
Don't cry to me when he doesn't make you his wife...

Your Love

Love fake as a game
Nothing said was ever real
You just want a name

Pieces Of A Heart

Together as one you hear a beat
Pieces working together to continue life
Red and blue flow through viciously
Trying to rebuild what is broken
Bandage after stab not helping
Flow irregular like two left feet
Beats slowly fading in the dust

Musical notes only savior
But when that music player dies,
What will be there to continue the beat...

Blast From The Past

Times have changed but this bond the same
Has she come to gain my name?
Only talk through satellite
Will this fire reignite?

Connection only ended because of space
But we definitely stopped in first place
If our hands reunite,
Will this fire reignite?

Back then we were both pure
And the goal was marriage: we were sure
Yet we had to step away from the limelight
Will this fire reignite?

Now grown and aware
Are we going somewhere?
No need to expedite but
Will this fire reignite?

Heart fading
Hope these words are persuading
Can you be Mrs. Right?
Let this fire reignite

Apology

Sorry that I ruined your day
And put a bad memory on replay
That was definitely foul play
Something I should not downplay
Please don't runaway
Everything happened yesterday
Don't let this bond decay
Just give me a chance and stay
Let me be better today

Broken

A Broken soul can prevail
Once you learn to pass the storm.
Life takes you where you will fail
But you still have to perform

Even after everything is lost,
A Broken soul can prevail
The strength needed to overcome has no cost
Look within to unveil

Your mind is the killer whale
You have to overcome all your fears
A Broken soul can prevail
No matter how impossible it appears

You are in control of your outcome
Nobody has to know you are feeling frail
People only need to see you overcome
A Broken soul can prevail

www.ingramcontent.com/pod-product-compliance
Lightning Source LLC
Chambersburg PA
CBHW061328040426
42444CB00011B/2820